E CLASSICS

Great American
Short Stories II

Richard Harding
DAVIS

Stories retold by C.D. Buchanan
Illustrated by James Balkovek

LAKE EDUCATION
Belmont, California

LAKE CLASSICS

Great American Short Stories I

Washington Irving, Nathaniel Hawthorne, Mark Twain, Bret Harte, Edgar Allan Poe, Kate Chopin, Willa Cather, Sarah Orne Jewett, Sherwood Anderson, Charles W. Chesnutt

Great American Short Stories II

Herman Melville, Stephen Crane, Ambrose Bierce, Jack London, Edith Wharton, Charlotte Perkins Gilman, Frank R. Stockton, Hamlin Garland, O. Henry, Richard Harding Davis

Great British and Irish Short Stories

Arthur Conan Doyle, Saki (H. H. Munro), Rudyard Kipling, Katherine Mansfield, Thomas Hardy, E. M. Forster, Robert Louis Stevenson, H. G. Wells, John Galsworthy, James Joyce

Great Short Stories from Around the World

Guy de Maupassant, Anton Chekhov, Leo Tolstoy, Selma Lagerlöf, Alphonse Daudet, Mori Ogwai, Leopoldo Alas, Rabindranath Tagore, Fyodor Dostoevsky, Honoré de Balzac

Cover and Text Designer: Diann Abbott

Library of Congress Catalog Number: 94-075031
ISBN 1-56103-023-6
Printed in the United States of America
1 9 8 7 6 5 4 3 2 1

CONTENTS

❦ Lake Classic Short Stories ❧

"The universe is made of stories, not atoms."

—Muriel Rukeyser

"The story's about you."

—Horace

Everyone loves a good story. It is hard to think of a friendlier introduction to classic literature. For one thing, short stories are *short*—quick to get into and easy to finish. Of all the literary forms, the short story is the least intimidating and the most approachable.

Great literature is an important part of our human heritage. In the belief that this heritage belongs to everyone, *Lake Classic Short Stories* are adapted for today's readers. Lengthy sentences and paragraphs are shortened. Archaic words are replaced. Modern punctuation and spellings are used. Many of the longer stories are abridged. In all the stories, painstaking care has been taken to preserve the author's unique voice.

Lake Classic Short Stories have something for everyone. The hundreds of stories in the collection cover a broad terrain of themes, story types, and styles. Literary merit was a deciding factor in story selection. But no story was included unless it was as enjoyable as it was instructive. And special priority was given to stories that shine light on the human condition.

Each book in the *Lake Classic Short Stories* is devoted to the work of a single author. Little-known stories of merit are included with famous old favorites. Taken as a whole, the collected authors and stories make up a rich and diverse sampler of the story-teller's art.

Lake Classic Short Stories guarantee a great reading experience. Readers who look for common interests, concerns, and experiences are sure to find them. Readers who bring their own gifts of perception and appreciation to the stories will be doubly rewarded.

🌿 Richard Harding Davis 🌿
(1864–1916)

About the Author

Richard Harding Davis was born in Philadelphia during the Civil War. His father was an editor, and his mother was a writer. No one was surprised when he too chose a literary life.

Davis was a fancy dresser. He was sometimes called the Beau Brummel of the Press. But this mocking nickname is misleading, for Davis was a very skilled and brave reporter. He always got close to the action, no matter how dangerous it might be.

Davis covered stories all over the world and reported on many wars. He spoke to generals as if they were his friends. Although the rules of war did not allow it, he took part in the Battle of San Juan Hill during the Spanish-American War.

During World War I, he tried very hard to get in on the action. Once he was almost shot as a spy by the Germans. Other reporters said that no war was quite first-rate unless Davis was there to write about it.

When he wasn't reporting on wars, Davis covered other news events. He was paid $500—a lot of money at the time—to report on a Yale-Princeton football game. He is remembered as an interesting character who liked to do things with flair. At one time, he had a messenger travel 8,000 miles to deliver a ring to his fiancée. He sent daily reports to the press on the messenger's progress.

Davis's stories are set all over the world. His characters became the standard for the ideal male of the time. This "ideal male" was tall, handsome, brave, and constantly on the go. He was good to the poor and unfortunate. And his manners were perfect.

If you like stories about handsome heroes in dangerous situations, you'll enjoy reading Richard Harding Davis.

The Deserter

A famous football coach once said that "Fatigue makes cowards of us all." Do you agree with him? This dramatic story is about a man who has reached his limits. Brought down by exhaustion, he can see only one way out. But has he thought through the consequences of what he is about to do?

"WHAT DO YOU SUPPOSE I'M HIDING IN YOUR ROOM
FOR—SO I WON'T CATCH COLD?"

The Deserter

Salonika is a port city in Greece. In 1917, only a few Americans were living there. The whole American colony was made up of the American consul, the man from Standard Oil, and the war correspondents, or reporters. The world was in the middle of "the great war." The correspondents were waiting to go to the front, where all the action was. The real war news was out there.

There were four of us reporters. "Uncle" Jim had seen many wars. Of our group, he was the oldest in experience, but the youngest in spirit. Then there was the Kid, and the Artist.

The Kid made fun of us. He liked to describe himself as a Boy Reporter. He often bragged about jumping from a City Hall desk to cover a European War. "I don't know military strategy," he would boast. "But neither does the Man at Home. He wants to read 'human interest' stuff, and I give him what he wants. I write for the folks on the subway and the farmers in the wheat belt.

"When you fellows write about 'the Situation,' the ordinary people don't understand it. Neither do you. I don't understand it myself. So, I write heart-to-heart stories about refugees and the wounded for my people. I tell them what kind of plows the farmers use. I tell them to pronounce Salonika, *sal-on-eeka*.

"You fellows write for the editorial page—and nobody reads it. I write for the man who reads the comics first, and then looks to see what the new movies are. When that man has to choose between reading either 'our military correspondent' or the City Hall Reporter, he chooses me!"

The third reporter was John. We called him "Our Special Artist." John could write a news story, too. But it was his cartoons that had made him famous. They were not comic page stuff, but front page cartoons. Before making up their minds about what they thought, readers waited to see what their Artist thought. So it was a good thing that John's thoughts were as brave and clean as they were clever.

John had a special feeling for the poor. He was always giving away money. When we caught him at it, he would make up excuses. He might say that the man was a college pal. Or he might say that he was only paying back money he had borrowed. The Kid said it was strange that so many of John's college pals turned up at the same time. And all of them were dead broke in Salonika!

John smiled. "It was a large college," he explained.

There were other Americans in Salonika, trying to get back to the United States. Many of them had no place to sleep, or wash, or change their clothes. Some didn't have clothes to change. We reporters were ranked as residents *because* we had clothes to change, and a hotel bedroom, instead of a bench in a cafe. The Greek police had given us official permission to stay in Salonika.

Our American colony was very close. We were only six Americans among thousands of soldiers and civilians from dozens of different countries. We reporters had arrived in Salonika before the rush. Right away we had rented a huge room at a waterfront hotel.

The harbor was right under our noses. We saw everybody who arrived on the Greek passenger boats. Everyone who came ashore from a warship or hospital ship was captured by our cameras. In our room, there were four windows—one for each of us and his work table.

It was not easy to work there. What was the use? The pictures and stories outside our windows were wonderful, of course. But we had no facts. Our stories showed how little we really knew about the war.

All day long, ships and passengers came and went from the harbor. The wounded were taken off the ships and loaded into ambulances. Sometimes a coffin was carried up the stone steps, while marines stood at salute. The harbor was so crowded that the oars of the boatmen sometimes locked together.

Beyond this busy scene rose the snow-draped shoulders of Mount Olympus. We often wondered how the ancient Greek gods and goddesses could stand the cold up there. Was Mount Olympus only their summer resort?

Before long, people found out that we had a huge room to ourselves. It became known that a visitor might find a drink there, or a bed for the night. So, we had many strange visitors. Some were half starved, or half frozen. They had terrible tales to tell. We heard of the Austrian prisoners who had fallen by the wayside of the mountain passes piled with dead.

We heard about the doctors and nurses wading through waist-high snowdrifts.

Some of our visitors wanted to get their names in the American papers. They wanted to let the folks at home know they were still alive. Others wanted us to keep their names *out* of the papers. Their hope was that the police would think they were dead.

All of us were hungry for real news to report. But we had to make do with rumors. Each of us had his "scouts" to bring rumors from the bazaar, the Turkish bath, and the cafes. Some of our scouts journeyed far up into the mountains. When they returned, they dripped snow on the floor and told us tales. Half of their stories we refused to believe. The other half the censor refused to let us send.

We all understood that the polite thing was not to interfere with each other's visitors. It would have been like listening in on a private telephone conversation. We said nothing if we found John drawing a giant stranger in a cap and

coat of wolf skin. We did not ask who the
visitor was. If a mysterious stranger sat
close to the Kid, whispering—while the
Kid banged on his typewriter—we did
not listen.

So I asked no qustions the afternoon I
found a strange American fellow writing
at John's table. John did not introduce
us, and I did not introduce myself. But I
could not help hearing what they said. I
tried to drown their voices by beating on
the Kid's typewriter. I was taking my
third typing lesson. I had just written,
"I AMM writjng This 5wjth my own
handS," when I heard the Kid say:

"You can get out this way. Let John buy
you a ticket to the Piraeus. If you go from
one Greek port to another, you don't need
a visa. But if you book from here to Italy,
it's a different story. Then you must get
a permit from the Italian consul, our
consul, *and* the police.

"Your idea is to get out of the war zone,
isn't it? Well, then, let's get you out quick.
You can plan the rest of your trip when
you're safe in Athens."

It was no business of mine, but I had to look up. The stranger was now pacing the floor. I noticed that his face was deeply tanned, but his upper lip was quite white. I also noticed that he wore one of John's blue suits, and a pink silk shirt that belonged to the Kid. There was nothing unusual in the young man's appearance. He looked like an American businessman or perhaps an insurance agent.

John picked up his hat and said, "That's good advice. Give me your steamer ticket, Fred, and I'll have them change it." Then he went out. I had no idea why he did not ask Fred to go with him.

Uncle Jim stood up. He said something about the Cafe Roma, and tea. But he did not invite Fred to go with him, either. Instead, he told Fred to make himself at home. If he wanted anything, the waiter would bring it from the cafe downstairs. Then the Kid, too, hurried to the door. "Going to get you a suitcase," he explained. "I'll be back in five minutes."

The stranger made no answer. Probably he did not hear him. Not a hundred feet from our windows three Greek steamers were huddled together. The American's eyes were fixed on those steamers. The ship on which John had gone to buy him a new ticket lay nearest. She was to sail in two hours.

For some time the stranger paced the room in silence. Then the noise I was making on the typewriter disturbed him. He stopped pacing and watched my struggle. "You a newspaper man, too?" he asked. I said that I was. Then I begged him not to judge me by my typewriting.

"I got some great stories to write when I get back to God's country," he announced. "Before the war, I was a reporter for two years in Kansas City. Now I'm going back to teach and write. I got enough material to keep me busy for five years. All kinds of stuff—specials, stories, personal experiences, maybe a novel."

I looked at him with envy. So far, the pickings had been slim for the rest of us news hounds in the greatest of all wars. "You are to be congratulated," I said sincerely.

"For what?" he demanded. "I didn't go after the stories. They came to me. The things I saw, I *had* to see. Couldn't get away from them. I've been with the British, serving in the Royal Army Medical Corps. I've been a hospital orderly, stretcher bearer, and an ambulance driver. For 16 months I've been at the front—all that time on the firing-line. I've seen more of this war than any soldier. Sometimes they give the soldier a rest. They *never* give the medical corps a rest. The only rest I got was when I was wounded."

I looked him over closely. He seemed no worse for his wounds. Again I offered him congratulations. This time he accepted them. The memory of the things he had seen had stirred him. Now he talked on and on—not boastfully, but in a tone of wonder and disbelief. It was as if he were trying to make himself believe that these things really happened.

"I don't believe there's any kind of fighting I haven't seen," he declared. "Hand-to-hand fighting with bayonets, grenades, gun butts. I've seen 'em on their knees in the mud, choking each other. I've seen 'em beating each other with their bare fists. I've seen every kind of airship, bomb shell, poison gas, and every kind of wound.

"I've watched whole villages being turned into a brickyard in 20 minutes. In Serbia, I saw bodies of women frozen to death, bodies of babies starved to death. In Belgium, I saw men swinging from trees. Along the Yzer River, I saw the bodies of men I'd known. Some of them were sticking out of the mud. Some were hung up on the barbed wire, with the crows picking at them.

"I've seen some of the nerviest stunts that were ever pulled off in history. I've seen *real* heroes. Time and again I've seen a man throw away his life for his officer—or for someone he didn't even know. I've seen women nurses steer a car into a village to yank out a wounded man. And all the while, shells were breaking under their wheels. Not to mention the houses that were pitching into the streets!" He stopped and laughed.

"Understand," he warned me, "I'm not talking about *myself*—only of things I've seen. The things I'm going to put in my book. It ought to be a pretty good book, don't you think?"

Admiration had washed away my envy.

"It will make a wonderful book," I agreed. "Are you going to run it in the magazines first?"

Young Mr. Hamlin frowned importantly.

"I was thinking," he said. "Maybe I should ask John for letters to the magazine editors. So they'll know I'm not faking—that I've really been through it all. Letters from John would help a lot." Then he asked anxiously, "They would, wouldn't they?"

I told him they would. "Are you another college pal of John's?" I asked. The young man answered quite seriously. "No," he said. "John graduated before I entered.

But we belong to the same fraternity. Finding him here was the luckiest chance in the world. I could hardly believe it when I read in the *Balkan News* that he was in Salonika. I asked for 12 hours' leave and came down in an ambulance. Then I made straight for John. I gave him the secret fraternity handshake, and asked him to help me."

"I don't understand," I said. "I thought you were sailing on the *Adriaticus*?"

The young man was again pacing the floor. He stopped and looked out at the harbor.

"You bet I'm sailing on the *Adriaticus*," he said, grinning. "In just two hours!"

I suppose it was stupid of me, but I still couldn't understand. "But what about your 12 hours' leave?" I asked.

The young man laughed. "They can take my 12 hours' leave and feed it to the chickens. I'm beating it."

"What do you mean, you're beating it?"

"What do you suppose I mean?" he demanded. "What do you suppose I'm doing out of uniform? What do you suppose I'm hiding in your room for—so I won't catch cold?"

"If you're leaving the army without permission," I said, "I suppose you know it's desertion."

Mr. Hamlin laughed easily. "It's not *my* army," he said. "I'm an American."

"But it's your desertion," I suggested.

The door opened and closed noiselessly. Billy entered and placed a new suitcase on the floor. He must have heard my last word, for he looked inquiringly at each of us. But he did not speak. Walking to the window, he stood with his hands in his pockets. He stared out at the harbor.

The young man continued. "Who knows I'm deserting?" he demanded. "No one's ever seen me in Salonika before. And in these clothes, I can get on board ship all right. Then they can't touch me.

"What do the folks at home care *how* I left the British army? They'll just be glad to get me back alive. No one will ask if I walked out or was kicked out. I should worry!"

"It's none of my business—" I began, but I was interrupted. In his restless pacing, the young man turned on me quickly.

"As you say," he said, in a voice like ice. "It *is* none of your business. It's none of your business whether I get shot as a deserter, or go home, or—"

"You can do whatever you like," I assured him. "I wasn't really thinking of *you* at all. I was only sorry that I'll never be able to read your book."

For a moment Mr. Hamlin was silent. Then he shouted, "No British firing squad will ever get *me*!"

"Maybe not," I agreed, "but you will never write that book."

Again there was silence. This time it was broken by the Kid. He turned from the window and looked toward Hamlin.

"That's right!" he said.

He sat down on the edge of the table. Then he pointed at the deserter.

"Son," he said, "this war is some war. It's the biggest war in history. Folks will be talking about nothing else for the next 90 years. But you won't talk about it. And you've been through it all. But *you* won't be able to talk about this war—or teach, or write a book about it."

"I won't?" demanded Hamlin. "And why won't I?"

"Because of what you're doing now," said Billy. "Because you're ruining yourself. Right now, you've got just about everything." The Kid was very much in earnest. His tone was quiet, kind, and friendly. "You've seen everything and done everything.

"Reporters like us would give our eye-teeth to see what you've seen. We'd give anything to write the things you can write. You've got a good record now. That will last you until you're dead, and your grandchildren are dead—and then some. When you talk, the folks back home will have to sit up and listen.

"You can say, 'I was there. I was in it. I saw. I know.' When this war is over, you'll have everything out of it that's worth getting. You'll have all the experiences, all the inside knowledge, all the news. You'll have wounds, honors, medals, money, reputation. And you're throwing all that away!"

Mr. Hamlin shouted out savagely.

"I don't want their medals," he cried. "They can take their medals and hang 'em on a Christmas tree. I don't owe the British army anything. It owes *me*. I've done *my* bit. I've earned what I've got, and there's no one can take it away from me."

"*You* can," said the Kid. But before Hamlin could reply, the door opened and John came in, followed by Uncle Jim. The older man was looking very grave, and John very unhappy. Hamlin turned quickly to John.

"I thought these men were friends of yours," he snorted. "And Americans. They're *fine* Americans! They're as full of human kindness and red blood as a dead fish!"

John looked inquiringly at the Kid.

"He wants to hang himself," explained Billy. "Because we tried to cut him down, he's mad."

"They talked to me," protested Hamlin, "as though I was a coward. As though I was a quitter. I'm no quitter! But, if I'm ready to quit—who's got a better right? I'm not an Englishman. And there are several million Englishmen who haven't done as much for England in this war as I have.

"What do you fellows know about it? You *write* about it, about the 'brave lads in the trenches.' But what do you really know about the trenches? Only what you've seen from automobiles. That's all. I've *lived* in the trenches for 15 months. I froze in 'em, starved in 'em, risked my life in 'em. And I've saved lives, too, by hauling men out of the trenches. And that's no hot air, either!"

Then Hamlin ran to the closet where John's clothes were hung. From the bottom of it, he dragged a khaki uniform that was still caked with mud and snow.

When he threw it on the floor, it splashed like a wet bathing suit. "How would you like to wear one of *these*?" he demanded. "Stinking with lice and sweat and blood. The blood of the men you've helped off the field, and your own blood as well."

He drew his hand across his stomach, and then from his waist to his chin. "I'm scraped with shrapnel from there to there," said Mr. Hamlin. "Another time I got shot in the shoulder. They would have given a fighting man leave for that. But all I got was six weeks in the hospital.

"After that it was the Dardanelles, in Turkey. Sunstroke and sand. Sleeping in sand, eating sand, sand in your boots, sand in your teeth. Hiding in holes in the sand like a prairie dog. Then it was 'Off to Serbia!' That act opened in the snow and the mud! Cold? God, how cold it was! And most of us were in sun helmets."

As though the cold still gnawed at his bones, he shivered.

"It isn't the danger," he protested. It isn't *that* I have to get away from. It's just the plain misery of it! It's never being your own master, never being clean, never being warm." Again he shivered and rubbed one hand against the other.

"There were no bridges over the streams," Hamlin went on. "We had to break the ice and wade in. Then we had to sleep in the open with our uniforms frozen to us. There was no firewood— not enough to warm a pot of tea. There were no wounded to carry along with us. All our victims died of frost bite and pneumonia. When we took them out of the blankets, their toes fell off.

"We've been in camp for a month now, and it's worse than on the march. It's a frozen swamp. You can't sleep for the cold. Can't eat. The only food we get is dried beef, and our insides are frozen so tight we can't digest it. The cold gets into your blood, your brains. It won't let you think. Or it makes you think crazy things. It makes you afraid." He shook himself like a man coming out of a bad dream.

"So, I'm through," he said. He glared at each of us, as if daring us to stop him. "That's why I'm quitting," he added. "Because I've done my bit. Because I'm fed up with it!" He kicked at the wet uniform on the floor. "Anyone who wants my job can have it right now!"

Hamlin walked to the window, and turned his back on us. His eyes were hungrily fixed on the *Adriaticus*. There was a long pause. We looked at John for help, but he was staring down at the desk blotter. Silently, he scratched marks on it that he did not see.

Finally the Kid jumped in. "That's certainly a hard luck story," he said. "But," he added cheerfully, "it's nothing to the hard luck you're *going* to have. Just wait until you can't tell why you left the army!"

Hamlin turned on them angrily, but Billy held up his hand. "Now wait," he begged, "we have no time to argue. At six o'clock your leave is up. The troop train starts back to camp then, and—"

"And the *Adriaticus* starts at five." Hamlin interrupted sharply.

Billy paid no attention. "You've got two hours to change your mind," he said. "That's better than being sorry you didn't for the rest of your life."

Hamlin threw back his head and laughed. It was a most unpleasant laugh. "You're a fine body of men," he jeered. "America must be proud of you!"

"If we weren't Americans," explained Billy patiently, "we wouldn't give a hoot whether you deserted or not. You're drowning—and you don't know it. We're throwing you a rope. Try to see it that way. We'll leave out the fact that you took an oath, and that you're breaking it. That's up to you.

"Let's get down to results. When you reach home, will you say why you left the army? If you won't tell, the folks will darned soon guess. And that will ruin everything you've done. When you want to sell your stories, it will ruin you with the editors, ruin you with the publishers.

"If they know you broke your word to the British army, how can they know you're telling them the truth? How can they believe anything you tell them? Every story you write, every statement you make will sound like a fake. You'll be licked before you start.

"This is what will happen to you. When you give a talk on your 'Fifteen Months at the British Front,' someone will stand up and say, 'I want to ask a question. Is it true that you deserted from the British army? If you return, will they really shoot you?'"

I was scared. I expected Hamlin to grab Billy and throw him on the floor with the soggy uniform. But instead he stood motionless. His arms were pressed across his chest. His eyes, filled with anger and distress, returned to the *Adriaticus.*

"I'm sorry," said the Kid.

John looked at us and pointed to the door. We escaped only too gladly. John followed us into the hall. "Let me talk to him," he whispered. "The boat sails in an hour. Please don't come back until she's gone."

We went to the movies. But I don't think any of us had our minds on the film. After an hour, we heard the long, drawn-out warning of a steamer's loud whistle. We nudged each other, then got up and went out.

Not a hundred yards from us, the *Adriaticus* was slowly moving to sea.

"Good-bye, Mr. Hamlin," called Billy. "You had everything and you threw it away."

But when we entered our room, there stood the deserter. He wore the dirty, water-soaked uniform. The sun helmet was on his head.

"Good man!" shouted Billy.

He walked forward, holding out his hand.

Hamlin brushed past him. At the door he turned and glared at us, even at John. He was not a good loser. "I hope you're satisfied," he snarled. He pointed at our four beds. They looked so soft they made me ashamed.

"I hope you'll think of me in the mud," said Hamlin, "when you turn into those beds tonight. When you're having your five-course dinner, and your champagne, I hope you'll remember my dried beef. When a shell or Mr. Pneumonia gets me, I hope you'll write a nice little sob story about the 'brave lads in the trenches.'"

He stared at us. We stood as silent as sheepish schoolboys. Then he threw open the door. "I hope," he added, "that you all choke!"

We heard the door slam and his boots pound down the stairs. No one spoke. Instead, in unhappy silence, we stood staring at the floor. Where the uniform had lain, there was a puddle. It was a pool of mud and melted snow and the darker stains of old blood.

The Consul

How far would you bend the rules in order to save your career? The main character in this story is threatened by one of the most powerful men in government. Will the tired old man stick to his principles, or will he back down?

"I REFUSE TO PLACE THE SEAL OF THIS CONSULATE ON A LIE."

The Consul

For over 40 years, in one part of the world or another, old man Marshall had served his country. As the official American representative to foreign countries, his title was United States Consul. He had been appointed to this office by Abraham Lincoln.

This fact had saved his career many times, when eager young politicians wanted his position. It was as if the ghost of the dead president still protected him. In the State Department, Marshall had become a tradition. "You can't touch *him*!" the State Department would say. "Why, *he* was appointed by Lincoln!"

Secretly, the State Department was grateful to have this weapon to protect Old Man Marshall. He was the kind of diplomat the department loved. Like a true soldier, he was obedient and disciplined. Wherever he was sent— there, without question, he would go. No matter how bad the conditions might be, he never complained.

He had an excellent record. The reports he turned in were models of good English. They were full of information, intelligent, and valuable. Just a few Americans ran across him these days. Lately he had been banished to out-of-the-world places. But everyone who met him spoke of him with admiration and even awe. He had never asked to be promoted. Though he had few friends left anymore, the State Department could not ignore his record. And his connection with the dead president was still honored. So even though he was never promoted—he was not dismissed, either.

Porto Banos, of the Republic of Colombia, was Mr. Marshall's current post. One could find little good to say about this small town, except that it has a fine harbor. In stormy weather on the Caribbean, even large war-ships could find safety in Porto Banos' harbor. But, as young Mr. Aiken, the wireless operator, pointed out—that didn't count for much. No one ever visited Porto Banos, unless driven by a hurricane.

The town consisted of rows of huts with grass roofs, dirt roads, and a few poor buildings. And then there were the white-washed adobe houses of the consuls. The back yard of the whole town was a swamp. At five each morning, a rusty engine pulled a train to the base of the mountains. At five in the evening, the same train came back, loaded with filled coffee-sacks. This going and coming happened every day, if the train rails did not sink into the swamp.

In the daily life of Porto Banos, waiting for the return of the train was the chief interest. People even made bets on the time it would return. Each night the consuls, the foreign residents, the

wireless operator, and the manager of
the rusty railroad met for dinner. Mr.
Marshall was the chosen ruler of this
little band of exiles. His rule was gentle.
His fine example had made living in
Porto Banos more bearable for everyone.

Before Mr. Marshall came, the
residents had lost interest. They had
grown lazy, bad-tempered, and unhappy.
Their white uniforms were seldom white.
Their faces were unshaven. They drank
too much, gambled, and quarreled.

But Mr. Marshall changed all that. His
own high standards, his kindness, and
his wisdom were a good example for
everyone. His cheerful courtesy and
personal neatness made the younger
men ashamed. Their desire to please him
brought back their pride and self-esteem.
His good opinion was important to them.

An officer from a British ship noticed
the change. "Used to be," he said, "you
couldn't get out of the Cafe Bolivar
without someone sticking a knife in you.
Now it's a debating club. Who would
believe it? Now they all sit around and

listen to an old gentleman talk about world affairs."

Henry Marshall indeed brought happiness to the poor exiles of Porto Banos. But there was little that Porto Banos could give to him in return. He had newspapers in six languages sent to him every week. They kept him in touch with the foreign lands where he had once represented his country. But newspapers and magazines from his own country were no comfort. They showed him only too clearly that in 40 years the United States had changed beyond recognition.

Henry Marshll had not forgotten the last time he had visited the State Department. The new young crowd there had made him feel like a man without a country. When he visited his home town in Vermont, he was treated as an ancient old-timer. Most of his boyhood friends were dead. Many of those who were still living thought that he was dead. The sleepy, pretty village had become a busy commercial center. Where he had once walked among wheatfields, trolley-cars now whirled between rows of mills and factories.

Like a ghost, he searched for house after house, where once he had been made welcome. In the place of every house, he found a towering office building. As the song goes, "All had gone, the old familiar faces." In his own home, he was a stranger among strangers. In the service he had so faithfully followed, rank by rank, he had been dropped. Twice he had been a consul-general. Now he was an exile—banished to a fever swamp. The great Ship of State had "marooned" him and sailed away.

Twice a day the old man walked along the shell road to the Cafe Bolivar, and back again to his office. There, as he entered, the Colombian clerk would rise and bow.

"Any papers for me to sign, Jose?" the consul would ask.

"Not today, Excellency," the clerk would reply. In the inner office, the consul would gaze at the empty harbor.

He had little to do but study the empty coral reefs and the empty, burning sky.

As usual, the little band of exiles were at breakfast one morning. Then suddenly, the radio operator rushed in. He announced that he had just heard a report that a hurricane was coming. The report also said that a yacht called *Serapis* was missing at sea.

For 48 hours, nothing had been heard from *Serapis*. It was believed she had been sunk by the hurricane. Much concern was felt in Washington. It happened that a Senator Hanley—the closest friend of the new president—was on board. In fact, many believed it was Senator Hanley who had most helped the new president to be elected.

The navy cruiser *Raleigh*, commanded by Admiral Hardy, had been ordered from Colon. Its mission was to try to make contact with *Serapis*. The navy thought it was possible that *Serapis* would seek shelter at Porto Banos. The consul was ordered to report.

As Marshall wrote out his answer, the French consul looked on with interest.

"He is important, this Senator Hanley? Is that what they do in your country? Are ships of war like the *Raleigh* at the service of a senator?" the French consul asked.

Aiken, the wireless operator, grinned.

"They are at the service of *this* senator," he answered. "Back at home they call Hanley 'the king-maker'—the man behind the throne."

"But in your country, there *is* no throne," said the Frenchman. "I thought your president was elected by the people?"

"That's what the people think," answered Aiken. "But rich people in the United States want a rich man in the Senate. They want their interests protected. They chose Hanley. And he chose the candidate for president that he thought would help the interests of the rich. Hanley nominated the candidate, and the people voted for him. Hanley is what we call a 'boss.'"

The confused Frenchman looked at Marshall.

"The position of the 'boss' is dangerous," said Marshall, "because it is not official. There are no laws to limit his powers. Men like Senator Hanley are a threat to good government. They see a public office only as a reward for their party workers."

"That's right," agreed Aiken. "Your 40 years of service wouldn't mean a thing to Hanley. What do you think he would do if he wanted your job for himself or for one of his workers? He'd throw you out as quick as he would a drunken cook."

"Oh, dear," sighed the French consul. "Then, let us pray that the hurricane has sunk the *Serapis* and all on board."

Two hours later the *Serapis* steamed into the harbor of Porto Banos.

The weather-beaten yacht showed that she had met the hurricane and had come out second best.

Her owner was one young Herbert Livingstone, of Washington, D.C. At one time, he had held the office of minister to The Netherlands. Now he wanted that office back. In order to bring this about, he had given a great deal of money to help elect the new president.

Livingstone had worked hard to convince Senator Hanley to come on this cruise. That alone showed Livingstone's ability as a diplomat. Many felt that this success would quickly lead to Livingstone's appointment as a minister. Livingstone certainly thought so.

The ambitious young man had lived in the nation's capital all of his life. He knew very well the value of being on the scene. Many men that he knew held important government jobs—simply because they belonged to the same clubs as men high in the government.

Livingstone was certain that three weeks on board his floating palace would impress Senator Hanley. After this, Hanley would not be able to refuse him even a prize post in Europe. As yet, Livingstone had not hinted at his ambition. But there was no need. Hanley was a keen statesman. To a man like him, the amount of money Livingstone had given to the campaign fund told its own story.

After their wrestling match with the hurricane, the guests on board the *Serapis* were happy to be on land. Even the swampland of Porto Banos looked good to them. Before the anchors even hit the water, they were in the launch. On reaching shore, they rushed straight to the consul's office. They all wanted to send telegrams. Every one of them had messages to send to their friends, to newspapers, to the government.

Old Henry Marshall and Jose, the Colombian clerk, seemed to be everywhere at once—eager and helpful. At Jose's desk stood the great senator himself. To Jose's joy, he was using Jose's own pen to write a message to the White House. At the consul's desk was a beautiful woman, dressed in lace and pearls. She was struggling to describe the hurricane in the ten words allowed for telegrams. Henry Cairns, the banker, was writing instructions to his Wall Street office. Livingstone himself had taken on the task of answering the newspaper inquiries heaped upon Marshall's desk.

It was just before sunset, and Marshall brought out his tea things. The beautiful woman, who was Miss Cairns, made tea for the women. The men mixed gin and limes with warm water. The consul gave a toast to those who had escaped the dangers of the sea. If they had been his oldest friends, his little speech could not have been more heart-felt and sincere. To his distress, one of the ladies burst into tears. Embarrassed, he turned to the men.

"I regret there is no ice," he said. "But you know the rule of the tropics: As soon as a ship enters port, the ice-machine breaks."

"I'll have some sent from the *Serapis*, sir," said Livingstone, the yacht owner. "And, as long as we're here—"

Senator Hanley gasped. "As long as we're here?"

"Not over two days," Livingstone answered, in a quick, nervous voice. "The chief says it will take that long to get *Serapis* in shape. As you ought to know, Senator, she was pretty badly damaged."

The senator gazed blankly out the window. Beyond it lay the naked coral reefs, the empty sky, and the ragged palms of Porto Banos.

Livingstone felt his ministry slipping away from him.

"The wireless operator," he went on, "tells me there is an interesting place a few miles down the coast. It's called Las Bocas—a sort of amusement park. The government people go there for the summer. There's good swimming, and nightclubs, and some Spanish dancers—"

The guests of the *Serapis* looked up with great interest. The senator smiled. To Marshall, their excitement over the thought of a ride on a merry-go-round was amazing. It suggested that Mr.

Livingstone's friends must not find each other's company very satisfying.

Livingstone continued. "And that wireless man said that we can get there in half an hour with the launch. Suppose we run down there after dinner?"

He turned to Marshall.

"Will you join us, Mr. Consul?" he asked, "and dine with us first, of course?"

Marshall accepted with pleasure. It had been many months since he had sat at table with people from his own country. But he shook his head.

"I was wondering about Las Bocas," he explained. "Going there might get you in trouble at the next port. With a yacht, it may be different. But Las Bocas is under quarantine—"

Everyone cried out in dismay.

"It's not serious," Marshall explained. "At one time there was bubonic plague there, or something like it. You would be in no danger from that now. It's only that you might be held up by their rules and regulations.

"Passenger steamers can't land anyone who has been there at any other port in the West Indies. The English are especially strict. The *Royal Mail*, for example, won't let just anyone on board here. Every passenger must have a certificate from the English consul saying he has not visited Las Bocas. For an American, they would require the same certificate from me.

"But I don't think the rules apply to yachts. I will find out. I don't wish to prevent you from going to Porto Banos," he added. "But I would blame myself if you were not allowed to land at your next port."

"It's all right," declared Livingstone. "Just as you say, the regulations don't include yachts. Besides, I carry my own doctor. If he won't give us a clean bill of health, I'll make him walk the plank. Dinner at eight, then! I'll send the launch for you."

The party from the yacht left their consul in a most friendly spirit.

"I think he's charming!" exclaimed Miss Cairns. "And did you notice his books? They were in every language. It must be terribly lonely down here for a man like that."

"This place makes me think of a postmaster in my state," Senator Hanley said. "He wants us to find him a post in the tropics as a consul. I'll tell him I've seen Porto Banos, and that it's just the place for him."

"What would become of Mr. Marshall?" asked Miss Cairns.

"I wasn't thinking of Mr. Marshall," the senator answered. "I can't recall that he has done anything for the president or our party." Turning to Miss Cairns, Hanley spoke in the tone he would use with a small child. "You see, Miss Cairns, Marshall has been living abroad for 40 years. All those years at the expense of the taxpayers! Some of us think that men in his position had better come home and get to work."

Livingstone nodded in agreement. As for himself, he did not wish a post abroad at the expense of the taxpayers. He was willing to pay for it himself. What he wanted was the title "ex-Minister" printed on his visiting cards. Then he would feel he had earned the right to join the other Americans living in Paris.

Just before dinner, the navy cruiser *Raleigh* entered the harbor. For more than a day it had been searching for the *Serapis*. Now Admiral Hardy came to the yacht to call on the senator. There he greeted Marshall with loud cries of joy.

The two old gentlemen had been friends for 30 years. They had served together in many strange parts of the world. To each man, their unexpected meeting was a great piece of good luck.

Livingstone's guests had long since become bored with each other. Now they became quite interested in the talk of former days between the consul and the admiral. The two old friends stayed behind when the rest of the men departed for Las Bocas. The women insisted that Marshall and Admiral Hardy go on talking with them.

For Marshall, it was a wonderful evening. Being with his old friend among such pleasant ladies was a rare pleasure. It helped to wipe out the months of bitter loneliness, the sense of failure, his hurt at being neglected. In the moonlight, on the cool deck, the two friends sat telling stories about each other. They described many jolly adventures and kept their audience laughing.

In other stories, many famous names and glamorous places were mentioned. Mrs. Cairns and her daughter were surprised to learn that Marshall had held such important posts. Once he had been the consul-general at Marseilles, the great French port. The ladies could hardly help comparing the consul's distinguished past with his present, homely post. The village of Porto Banos was no more than a black streak in the night, a row of mud shacks.

Later in the evening Miss Cairns took Admiral Hardy to one side.

"Admiral," she began eagerly, "tell me about your friend. Why is he here?

Why don't they give him a place that is worthy of him? I've met many of our representatives abroad, and I know I've never met a better man. We simply cannot afford to waste men like Henry Marshall. Why, he's one of the most interesting men I've ever met! He's lived everywhere, known everyone. He's a distinguished man. Even I can see that he knows his work well—that he's a diplomat, born and trained. I believe that—"

The admiral interrupted with a growl.

"You don't have to tell *me* about Henry," he said. "I've known the man for over 25 years. If Henry got what he deserved, he surely wouldn't be a consul on this tiny coral reef. He'd be a minister in Europe.

"Look at me! Henry and I are the same age! When Lincoln sent Henry to Morocco as consul, he also started me off in the navy. Now I'm an admiral. Henry has twice my brains, and he's already been a consul-general. Yet here he is—back at the bottom of the ladder!"

"Why?" demanded the fascinated young woman.

"Because the navy is a *real* service and the consular service isn't. Men like Senator Hanley use the consular service to pay their debts. While Henry's been serving his country abroad, he's lost his friends, lost his 'pull.' Those politicians in Washington have no use for him.

"They don't realize that a consul like Henry can make millions of dollars for Americans. He can keep them from shipping goods where there's no market. And he can show them where there is a market."

The admiral snorted. "You don't have to tell *me* the value of a good consul. But those politicians don't understand that. They only see that he has a job worth a few hundred dollars—and they want it. If he doesn't have other politicians to protect him, they'll take his job."

Miss Cairns raised her head.

"Why don't you speak to the senator?" she asked. "Tell him you've known Consul Marshall for years—"

"Glad to do it!" exclaimed the admiral. "But Henry must not know. I know what he'd do if he thought anything was given to him except on his merits. He wouldn't take it."

"Then we won't tell him," said the eager young woman. But then she hesitated for a moment.

"What would happen if *I* spoke to Mr. Hanley?" she asked. "If I told him what I learned about Mr. Marshall tonight— do you think it would it have any effect?"

"Don't know how it will affect Hanley," said the admiral. "But if you asked *me* to make Henry a consul-general, I'd make him an *ambassador*."

Later in the evening, Hanley and Livingstone were seated alone on deck. The visit to Las Bocas had not been very amusing after all. But to Livingstone's relief, the senator was now in a good humor. He seemed to be in a lively, talkative mood.

"People have the *strangest* idea of what I can do for them!" he laughed. One of his favorite games was to pretend he had no authority. "They believe that I have only to wave a wand to get them anything they want. I thought I'd be safe from all that on board a yacht."

Livingstone squirmed nervously.

"But it seems," the senator went on, "that I'm at the mercy of a conspiracy. The women all want me to do something for this fellow Marshall. If they had their way, they'd send him to England's Court of St. James. And old Hardy is after me, too. He tackled me about Marshall just an hour ago. So did Miss Cairns.

"And then Marshall himself got hold of me. I thought he was going to tell me how wonderful he was, too! But he didn't. He told me that Hardy ought to be a vice-admiral."

Livingstone laughed. "They must have planned it between them," he said with a smile. "Each man agreed to put in a good word for the other. That's what *I* think."

There had been other moments during the cruise when Senator Hanley would have loved to drop his host overboard.

Now he bent forward and pretended to be very serious. "That's what *you* think, is it? Livingstone, you certainly are a great judge of men!"

The next morning, old man Marshall woke with a feeling of happiness. He hadn't had that feeling for a very long time. Now he tried to remember what change had come to him. Then he remembered. His old friend Hardy had returned. And several new friends had come into his life and welcomed him kindly.

The old man was no longer lonely. With that thought in mind, he ran to the window. He had not been dreaming! In the harbor lay the pretty yacht, alongside the stately, white-hulled war-ship. The American flag that flew from each boat brought warm tears to his eyes. For the moment his troubled spirit was soothed.

While Marshall was dressing, a sailor brought a note from the admiral. It invited him to tea on board the war-ship, with the guests of the *Serapis*. His old friend added that he was coming to lunch. He wanted Marshall to set aside time for a long talk. The consul agreed gladly. The day promised to be as happy as the night before.

By nine-thirty in the morning, Senator Hanley, Miss Cairns, and Livingstone were seated around Marshall's desk. Livingstone looked deeply unhappy. But the senator was smiling broadly. He greeted the consul with hearty good humor.

"I'm ordered home!" Senator Hanley announced gleefully. Then he remembered Livingstone. "I needn't say how sorry I am to give up my yachting trip— but orders are orders."

Marshall did not even try to hide his disappointment.

"I am so sorry you are leaving," he said. "*Selfishly* sorry, I mean. I hoped that you all would be here for several days."

Then Marshall looked at Livingstone. "I understood the *Serapis* was disabled," he said.

"She is," answered Hanley. "So's the *Raleigh*. But I've got to reach Kingston, Jamaica, by Thursday. A boat leaves there Thursday for New York. At first it looked as though I couldn't do it. But then I saw that the *Royal Mail* is due in here today. She can get to Kingston on Wednesday night. It's a great piece of luck! I hate to bother you with my troubles," the senator said pleasantly. "But the agent of the *Royal Mail* in this town won't sell me a ticket. At least not until you've put your seal to it, Marshall."

He held out a piece of paper.

Marshall took the paper, but he did not look at it. Instead, he gazed at the senator with troubled eyes. When he spoke, his tone was full of concern.

"It is most unfortunate," he said. "But I am afraid the *Royal Mail* will not take you on board. Because of Las Bocas," he explained.

"Because of Las Bocas?"echoed Hanley. "You don't really mean they'll refuse to take me? Just because I spent half an hour at the end of a wharf, listening to a squeaky gramophone?"

"Maybe the regulations have been changed," Marshall offered, hopefully. "I will talk to the captain of the *Royal Mail*, and tell him—"

"Why tell *him*? He doesn't know I've been to that place. All I need is a clean bill of health from you. You have only to sign that paper."

Marshall looked at the senator with surprise.

"But I *can't*," he said quietly.

"You can't? Why not?"

"Because this certificate says that you have *not* visited Las Bocas. Unfortunately, you *have* visited Las Bocas."

The senator stared at Marshall curiously. "Where does your loyalty lie? Are you going to be bound by the silly rules of an unimportant British colony? Or will you honor your oath to the President of the United States? He desires my presence in Washington."

Marshall smiled good-naturedly and shook his head.

"I'm afraid, Senator," he said, "that your way of putting it is hardly fair. Unfortunately, the question is one of fact. I will explain to the captain—"

"You will explain *nothing* to the captain!" shouted Hanley. "This matter concerns no one but our two selves. I am asking an American consul to assist an American citizen in trouble. Are you refusing to carry out the wishes of his President?"

Marshall looked at the senator with surprise and disbelief.

"Are you asking me to put my name to what is not so?" he said. "Are you serious?"

"That paper, Mr. Marshall," said Hanley, "is only a form—a piece of red tape. There's no more danger of my carrying the plague to Jamaica than of my carrying a bomb. You *know* that."

"I do know that," agreed Marshall. "You are the innocent victim of a rule that is most unfair to you. My own position," he added, "is not important. But you can believe that this is not easy. It is certainly no pleasure for me to be unable to help you."

Hanley was leaning forward, his hands on his knees. He watched Marshall closely.

"Then you refuse?" he said. "Why?"

Marshall gave Hanley a look of grave disapproval.

"You *know* why," he answered quietly. "It is impossible."

"Am I to understand," Hanley exclaimed, "that you are turning down the request of a United States Senator and of the President of the United States?"

On Marshall's desk was the little iron stamp of the consulate. Marshall laid his hand upon it. "I refuse," he corrected, "to place the seal of this consulate on a lie."

Miss Cairns clasped her hands unhappily and stared down at the floor. Livingstone snorted in protest. Hanley tapped his knuckles on Marshall's desk.

"You may be of some importance down here in this fever swamp," Hanley said to Marshall. "But in Washington, I am a very important man. Do you realize that I am a senator from a state with more than four million people? And do you understand that you are preventing me from serving those people?"

Marshall nodded.

"Please understand something," the old man said. "I may not be important in Washington, as you say. But in this fever swamp I am honored to represent 80 million people. As long as that consular sign is over my door, I don't intend to dishonor it. Not for you, or the President of the United States, or any one of those 80 million people."

Hanley laughed shortly and walked to the door. There he drew out his watch.

"Mr. Marshall," he said, "if the cable is working, I'll take your sign away from you by sunset."

Marshall remained silent. He bowed and sat down, showing no sign of the dismay he felt.

Miss Cairns was not taken in by the consul's calm manner. "What will you do?" she asked.

"I don't know," said Marshall simply. "I would rather have resigned. It's a prettier finish. After 40 years—to be dismissed by a cable! It's a poor way of ending it."

Miss Cairns rose and walked to the door. There she turned and looked back.

"I am sorry," she said.

An hour later the feelings of Admiral Hardy were expressed more directly.

"If Hanley comes on board my ship," roared the admiral, "I'll kill him!"

Marshall laughed. The loyalty of his old friend was never so welcome.

"You'll treat him with every courtesy," Marshall said. "The only satisfaction he gets out of this is to see that he has hurt me. We will not give him that satisfaction."

But Marshall found that hiding his pain was more difficult than he had thought. At tea time, he again met

Senator Hanley and the guests of the *Serapis* on board the *Raleigh*. Everything seemed to remind him that his career had come to an end. The sad faces of the women reflected his own sadness. Livingstone treated him rudely. And the big war-ship itself reminded him of better days. Back then, he had only to press a button, and dozens of war-ships would come at his bidding.

At five o'clock, there was an awkward moment. The *Royal Mail* passed out of the harbor on her way to Jamaica. Senator Hanley watched the ship's departure in silence.

Livingstone, standing at his side, spoke in a voice that was heavy with sympathy.

"Have they answered your cable, sir?"

"They have," said Hanley gruffly.

"Was it—was it satisfactory?"

"It *was*," said the senator.

"And when are you going to tell him?" Livingstone asked eagerly.

"Now!" said the senator.

The guests were leaving the ship in the admiral's launch.

"Mr. Marshall," the admiral called, when he saw that everyone was seated. "When I stop the launch at the ship, you will stand ready to receive the consul's salute."

Marshall had forgotten that. On leaving a war-ship, a consul was entitled to a seven-gun salute. If he had remembered, he would have insisted that the ceremony be left out. He knew that the admiral wished to show his loyalty. It was clear that his old friend wanted to pay him this honor in order to shame Hanley.

But the ceremony was no longer an honor. Now it only served to show what had been taken away from him. But it was too late to avoid it. The first of seven guns had roared from the bow. Marshall took his place at the gangway of the launch. His eyes were fixed on the flag, and his gray head was uncovered. He pressed his hat above his heart. He was determined that no one should see that he was suffering.

Another gun spat out a burst of white smoke. There was another echoing roar. Another and another followed. Marshall counted seven. Then, with a bow to the admiral, he backed from the gangway.

But then another gun shattered the hot, heavy silence. Marshall was confused. He thought he had counted wrong, and returned to his place. But then a ninth gun roared. He could not still be mistaken. He turned to his friend. The admiral's eyes were fixed on the war-ship.

Again a loud gunshot shattered the silence. Was it a joke? Were they laughing at him? Marshall glanced toward the others. They were smiling. Then it *was* a joke. Behind his back, something had to be going on. Only Livingstone looked as bewildered as he felt.

Then for the 13th time, the blast of a gun shook the swampland of Porto

Banos. Then—and not until then—did the flag crawl slowly from the mast-head. Mary Cairns burst into tears. But Marshall saw that everyone else, except Mary and Livingstone, was smiling. Even the sailors in charge of the launch were grinning over at him. He was surrounded by smiling faces. And then, against all regulations, three long, splendid cheers could be heard from the war-ship.

Marshall felt his lips shaking. Tears forced their way to his eyes. "Charles," he begged the admiral, "are they laughing at me?"

But before the admiral could answer, Senator Hanley eagerly scrambled forward. He grabbed Marshall's hand.

"Mr. Marshall," he cried out, "our president has great faith in Abraham Lincoln's judgment of men. This salute has been made at his orders. It means that this morning he appointed you as our new minister to the Netherlands. I'm one of those politicians who keeps his word. I told you I'd take your tin sign away from you by sunset. Now I've done it!"

Thinking About
the Stories

The Deserter

1. Many stories are meant to teach a lesson of some kind. Is the author trying to make a point in this story? What is it?

2. Compare and contrast at least two characters in this story. In what ways are they alike? In what ways are they different?

3. In what town, city, or country does this story take place? Is the location important to the story? Why or why not?

The Consul

1. Which character in this story do you most admire? Why? Which character do you like the least?

2. How important is the background of the story? Is weather a factor in the story? Is there a war going on or some other unusual circumstance? What influence does the background have on the characters' lives?

3. Does the main character in this story have an internal conflict? Does a terrible decision have to be made? Explain the character's choices.

8